AN
ESSAY ON GOVERNMENT

AN ESSAY ON
GOVERNMENT

by
JAMES MILL

with an Introduction by
ERNEST BARKER, Litt.D.
Fellow of Peterhouse, Cambridge, and
Professor of Political Science in the University of Cambridge

CAMBRIDGE
AT THE UNIVERSITY PRESS
1937

CAMBRIDGE
UNIVERSITY PRESS

University Printing House, Cambridge CB2 8BS, United Kingdom

Cambridge University Press is part of the University of Cambridge.

It furthers the University's mission by disseminating knowledge in the pursuit of education, learning and research at the highest international levels of excellence.

www.cambridge.org
Information on this title: www.cambridge.org/9781107594043

First published 1937
First paperback edition 2015

A catalogue record for this publication is available from the British Library

ISBN 978-1-107-59404-3 Paperback

CONTENTS

INTRODUCTION

JAMES MILL was a Scotsman, from the county of Angus, who was educated in Arts and Divinity at the University of Edinburgh (1790–1797), and then, after some preaching and a good deal of tutoring, left Scotland for London in the beginning of 1802, at the age of twenty-nine. Down to the year 1819, when he was appointed (after the publication of his *History of British India* two years previously) to a post in the India House, he earned what must have been a somewhat precarious living by the use of his pen. He married in 1805; and his eldest son, John Stuart Mill, was born in 1806. His interest lay in economic, political and social questions:[1] the earliest known publication bearing his name was an essay directed against bounties on the exportation of corn (1804). By 1808 he was writing articles for the *Edinburgh Review* on a wide range of social subjects; and in the same year he made the acquaintance of Jeremy Bentham, with whom he was closely, and indeed intimately, connected for

[1] But as a Utilitarian Mill was also, and fundamentally, interested in psychology and ethics; and perhaps his greatest work is his *Analysis of the Phenomena of the Human Mind*.

many years to come. The two lived together as neighbours in London, and for several years (between 1809 and 1818) Mill and his family stayed with Bentham in the country during the summer. There was a coolness between them in later years; but down to 1830 (when he moved to a villa in Kensington), Mill lived next door to Bentham, as his tenant, in what is now Queen Anne's Gate, and Mill's children played in Bentham's garden. This is only the outward and visible sign of a close intellectual connection, in which Mill cast himself for the role of disciple, but in which, as we shall see, he gave as well as received. But Mill had other friends and allies as well as Bentham. Joseph Hume, the radical and economical politician, who sat in parliament steadily from 1812 onwards, had been Mill's school-fellow in Scotland, and was his friend in London. Brougham, who came to London in 1803, had been Mill's fellow-student at Edinburgh and always continued in close relations with him. Ricardo and Francis Place both became connected with Mill about 1811: Ricardo, according to his son, was 'the dearest of his friends', and Place, besides managing his money affairs, drew him into collaboration in the busy politics of the constituency of Westminster, especially about 1818. Grote became an acquaintance, through Ricardo, about 1818, a little before the time

when Mill wrote the essay on Government.
When we reflect on all these acquaintances and
influences, we realize that the essay had a large
background of talk and discussion—talk and
discussion not only with other thinkers, but also
with statesmen and men of affairs.

Mill wrote the essay on Government for the
Supplement to the fifth edition of the *Encyclopaedia Britannica*, which was planned by Con-
stable in 1814 and finally completed in 1824.
It was one of a number of articles which he
contributed. Others dealt with Jurisprudence,
the Liberty of the Press, Prisons and Prison
Discipline, Colonies, the Law of Nations, and
Education; and there was also an article en-
titled 'Economists', which has some bearing on
the argument of the article on Government.
Writing for an Encyclopaedia, Mill was careful
not to be definitely partisan or one-sided: he
told the editor of the Supplement, in a letter of
September, 1819, 'You need be under no alarm
about my article *Government*: I shall say nothing
capable of alarming even a Whig, and he is
more terrified at the principles of good government than the worst of Tories'. The article was
completed and Mill received payment for it in
1820. In writing to thank the editor for his 'very
liberal enclosure', Mill reports an application
which has been made to him as to the article.

'Certain persons who think it calculated to disseminate very useful notions, and wish to give a stimulus to the circulation of them' have proposed 'to print (not for sale, but for gratis distribution) a thousand copies.' Permission was given by the editor for the reprint: Hume, Grote and others subscribed; and Mill's article was thus given a wider circulation than the Supplement to the Encyclopaedia would have afforded by itself. I cannot discover when the first reprint appeared, and I do not know whether it was a reprint only of the article on Government or contained some of the other articles also. By 1824 (to judge from a manuscript note in Lord Acton's copy) there had appeared what was possibly a second edition of the reprint; and this contains the articles on Jurisprudence, the Liberty of the Press and the Law of Nations as well as that on Government. Mill, in a letter of August 1825, speaks of the second reprint 'being all gone, and great demand remaining'. (He also mentions—and this is a very interesting fact —that his essays 'are the text-books of the young men of the Union at Cambridge'.[1]) It was not,

[1] A number of young men from Cambridge had joined the circle of James and John Stuart Mill about this time. They had taken up with James Mill's writings in their undergraduate days, and had used them in the debates of the Union—then, as J. S. Mill states in his Autobiography, 'at the height of its reputation...an arena where

apparently, till 1828 that a third reprint appeared. This contained three additional articles—those on Prisons, Education and Colonies—and it was this reprint that Macaulay had before him when he wrote a vigorous and brilliant attack on the essay on Government for the *Edinburgh Review* of March 1829.

Mill's Commonplace Book, which was presented by his son to the London Library, shows that he had read widely on the topic of Government. It contains 'citations from history' (which his critics accused him of neglecting) as well as 'from philosophers, statesmen and miscellaneous writers, directed against the mischiefs of unchecked authority and [in favour of] the necessity of representative institutions'[1]). Aristotle, Tacitus, Shaftesbury, Harrington, Turgot, Burke,

what were then thought extreme opinions, in politics and philosophy, were weekly asserted, face to face with their opposites, before audiences consisting of the élite of the Cambridge youth.' Prominent among the debaters had been Charles Austin, the brother of John Austin the jurist. When he came up to London from Cambridge, about 1822, he sought out the Mills, and introduced to them some of his distinguished Cambridge contemporaries. In this way James Mill, who had refused to send his son to Cambridge, and put him instead into the India House, was none the less brought into close connection with Cambridge men. These men played a large part in J. S. Mill's debating society after 1825, and helped in the spread of radical and utilitarian ideas.

[1] Professor Bain, *James Mill: a Biography*, p. 464.

Gibbon and Mackintosh are all used, especially
to point a moral against aristocracy. But the
great and primary source of Mill's ideas is the
talk and writings of his master, Jeremy Bentham.
When he wrote the article on Government he
had been in constant intercourse with Bentham
for a dozen years. It is true that, during these
dozen years, and even, indeed, from their very
beginning, he had been an active influence on
the thought of the master whom he believed that
he faithfully followed. Professor Halévy suggests
that it was the influence of Mill which contributed, in no small measure, to the change of
Bentham's opinions after 1808. He had long
been connected with the Tories: he had thought
that his principle of the greatest happiness of the
greatest number might be carried into effect (as
indeed it logically could be) by the beneficent
action of a superior authority, which identified
its own satisfaction with the satisfaction of that
principle. After thirty years of that way of
thinking he changed—partly under the influence
of the strain and stress of his own experience
(superior authority had not shown itself much
inclined to serve his principle or adopt his plans),
but partly, too, under the influence of the new
mind, with its democratic Scottish outlook,
which now stood at his side. Henceforth he
looked to the greatest number to achieve its own

happiness for itself: henceforth he relied on a system of representation, with annual parliaments, universal suffrage and a secret ballot, to check the selfishness of governments and secure the common interest. But if Mill had helped to start him along this new line of thought, he pursued it for himself, with all the fertility and all the originality of his own incessant thought; and before Mill wrote his essay on Government Bentham had written more than one work containing in essence, and in advance, the lines of thought, and even the terms and categories, which Mill was subsequently to follow and to use.[1] Prominent among these writings of Bentham was the 'Plan of Parliamentary Reform, in the form of a Catechism', which had been already begun in 1810, but was not finally published until 1817.[2] A comparison of this Plan (and more especially of the latter and shorter part which forms the catechism proper) with Mill's article of 1820 is sufficient to show the primary

[1] Yet it was Mill himself who, as Professor Halévy says, was 'the first of the Benthamites to base a theory of representative government on the principle of utility' (*The Growth of Philosophic Radicalism*, p. 257). One of his early articles for the *Edinburgh Review* (January 1809) deals with the republican constitutions of South America, and contains the same fundamental argument as the article on Government of 1820.

[2] The Plan is printed in Bowring's edition of *Bentham's Works*, Vol. III, pp. 433–557.

and immediate source of his argument. Another source, negative rather than positive, which deserves to be mentioned in passing, was an article in the *Edinburgh Review* of December 1818 by Sir James Mackintosh (author of the *Vindiciae Gallicae* and a considerable publicist), dealing with Bentham's Plan. In this article Mackintosh had expounded a theory of varied or functional representation, and it would seem to be Mackintosh's theory which Mill is criticizing—though he actually cites the authority of Lord Liverpool —at the end of the eighth section of his article.

Whatever Mill's sources were, and however deeply he was indebted to Bentham, his article rapidly became the classical statement of the political theory of the Benthamites. Bentham himself could not write briefly: rapid and fertile in argument, he hunted every hare and quartered every field that came into his view. Mill's succinct statement, which in the reprint formed a pamphlet of only 32 pages, was a ready vade mecum, and exercised an effect which was all the greater for its brevity. Conned by the young men of Cambridge, and debated in London clubs, it helped to precipitate opinion in the dozen years which preceded the passing of the first Reform Bill in 1832. Perhaps its spirit of positive dogmatism made it particularly trenchant and effective, though it also made it a little

less than just to the real temper and genius of
Bentham himself. Mill was a rigorous Scot,
endowed with a hard logic but destitute of the
peculiarly English humour of that 'comical old
fellow' (as he called himself) Jeremy Bentham;
nor had he his master's range and warmth of
sympathy. He gave a Pauline austerity to his
gospel: he hardened Bentham's opinions even
while he reproduced them; and in one particular
—his attitude to the rights of women (page 45)—
he lagged far behind Bentham, and offended the
opinion of his contemporaries. The general moral
theory of enlightened or reflective egoism which
underlies the article is identical with Bentham's
own 'self-preference principle': the conception
of a necessary conflict of interests between
governors and governed—a conception which
necessarily follows from the theory of egoism—
is also Bentham's conception: the idea that con-
flicting interests must be artificially identified,
and that representative government is the
sovereign way of identification—this, too, is
Bentham's idea. But while all—or nearly all—
of the theorems of Mill's article may be found
in Bentham, they have undergone a change. The
egoism is more egoistic: the negativism is more
negative. One can only say, in extenuation, that
the acid and corrosive quality of Mill's thought
was perhaps necessary in an age in which England

seemed a preserved estate of the aristocracy. *That* interest, at any rate, looked to itself: so Mill felt, and in that feeling he was not alone. Why should not other interests do the like—and in particular the interest of that 'most wise and most virtuous part of the community, the middle rank', all the more as it might be argued to comprehend the other interests? Here Mill becomes positive, and almost altruistic. Perhaps he also becomes inconsistent. It is difficult to be a complete egoist.

There were a number of contemporary attacks on the essay on Government. The most lively and the most trenchant, though it is in some places rhetorical and superficial, was the attack which Macaulay delivered in the *Edinburgh Review* of March 1829.[1] It was not the only attack which Macaulay delivered (though it is the one that most deserves to be read); another followed in the *Edinburgh Review* of June 1829, in answer to a rejoinder to his previous attack which had appeared, during the interval, in the *Westminster Review*, and which he thought had

[1] Macaulay, who had been at Cambridge with Charles Austin, had been introduced by him to James Mill. Though he criticized Mill's article on Government hotly, he had a high opinion of him (Bain, p. 456); and he used the argument of the first two paragraphs of the ninth section of the article in a speech in Parliament in 1831 (Halévy, pp. 421–422).

been written by Bentham himself: indeed a third attack was launched, in reply to a second rejoinder in the *Westminster Review*, before Macaulay's pen was exhausted (October 1829). Sir James Mackintosh also entered the lists, with the natural pugnacity of a Scot against an erring brother Scot, in the course of his *Dissertation on the Progress of Ethical Philosophy* (1830). This provoked the one answer which Mill made to his critics, the *Fragment on Mackintosh*. It is an answer to Macaulay as well as to Mackintosh. Mackintosh had acknowledged his sympathy with Macaulay's arguments; and Mill seizes on the acknowledgment to kill two birds with one stone.[1] There was one critic whom Mill was never able to answer. This was his own son, John Stuart Mill, who in his *System of Logic*, published in 1843, seven years after his father's death, examined the propriety and the justice of the method of argument followed in the essay on Government—the geometrical or abstract method (Book VI, chapter VIII).

It only remains to note that the article on Government is not the only contribution made by James Mill to the development of political theory. In the first appendix, at the end of this introduction, the reader will find a list of some of his other articles on political subjects, along

[1] *Fragment on Mackintosh*, pp. 275–294.

with a mention (which it seems only just to add) of some of his works in other fields, on which his reputation mainly depends. And if some things critical of his writings have here been said, let the testimony of Grote, a thinker as well as a historian, be set, in conclusion, on the other side of the account. 'Of all persons whom we have known Mr James Mill was the one who stood least remote from the lofty Platonic ideal of Dialectic—τοῦ διδόναι καὶ δέχεσθαι λόγον—competent alike to examine others, or to be examined by them, on philosophy. When to this we add a strenuous character, earnest convictions, and single-minded devotion to truth, with an utter disdain of mere paradox, it may be conceived that such a man exercised powerful intellectual ascendancy over younger minds.'[1]

APPENDIX I

A. Some of James Mill's articles on politics.

1. Articles in the *Edinburgh Review* on the Emancipation of South America, January and July 1809.

2. Articles for the Supplement to the *Encyclopaedia Britannica*, 1816–1823: final reprint, 1828.

[1] Quoted in Bain, p. 459.

3. Articles on the *Edinburgh* and the *Quarterly Reviews*, in No. 1 and No. 3 of the *Westminster Review*, 1824. (These articles examined the political views and attitude of the two *Reviews*.)

4. Article in the *Westminster Review* on the Ballot, July 1830.

5. Article on Aristocracy, *London Review*, January 1836.

B. Some of his articles on the Church.

(*a*) Article on Southey's *Book of the Church*, *Westminster Review*, January 1825.

(*b*) Article on Ecclesiastical Establishments, *Westminster Review*, April 1826.

(*c*) Article on the Church and its Reform, *London Review*, July 1835.

C. His published works.

(*a*) History of British India, 1817.

(*b*) Elements of Political Economy, 1821.

(*c*) Analysis of the Phenomena of the Human Mind, 1829.

(*d*) Fragment on Mackintosh (including a long vindication of Bentham and himself), 1835. (This was published anonymously. Section IV contains the vindication of Bentham.)

Appreciations and criticisms of Mill's views and writings, especially on politics.

(a) Macaulay, T. B. Articles in the *Edinburgh Review*, March, June and October 1829.

(b) Mackintosh, Sir James. Dissertation on the Progress of Ethical Philosophy, 1830.

(c) Mill, John Stuart. Autobiography (especially c. I–IV), 1873.

(d) Bain, A. James Mill: a Biography (especially c. V), 1882.

(e) Stephen, Leslie. The English Utilitarians, Vol. II (especially c. I–III), 1900.

(f) Halévy, E. The Growth of Philosophic Radicalism, English Translation (especially Part II, c. III, §§ 1 and 4; Part III, c. II, § 2; and c. III, § 2), 1928.

I

The End of Government; viz. the Good or Benefit for the Sake of which it exists

The question with respect to Government is a question about the adaptation of means to an end. Notwithstanding the portion of discourse which has been bestowed upon this subject, it is surprising to find, on a close inspection, how few of its principles are settled. The reason is, that the ends and means have not been analyzed; and it is only a general and undistinguishing conception of them, which is found in the minds of the greatest number of men. Things, in this situation, give rise to interminable disputes; more especially when the deliberation is subject, as here, to the strongest action of personal interest.

In a discourse, limited as the present, it would be obviously vain to attempt the accomplishment of such a task as that of the analysis we have mentioned. The mode, however, in which the operation should be conducted, may perhaps be described, and evidence enough exhibited to shew in what road we must travel, to approach the goal at which so many have vainly endeavoured to arrive.

The end of Government has been described in a great variety of expressions. By Locke it was said to be "the public good"; by others it has been described as being "the greatest happiness of the greatest number". These, and equivalent expressions, are just; but they are defective, inasmuch as the particular ideas which they embrace are indistinctly announced; and different conceptions are by means of them raised in different minds, and even in the same mind on different occasions.

It is immediately obvious, that a wide and difficult field is presented, and that the whole science of human nature must be explored, to lay a foundation for the science of Government.

To understand what is included in the happiness of the greatest number, we must understand what is included in the happiness of the individuals of whom it is composed.

That dissection of human nature which would be necessary for exhibiting, on proper evidence, the primary elements into which human happiness may be resolved, it is not compatible with the present design to undertake. We must content ourselves with assuming certain results.

We may allow, for example, in general terms, that the lot of every human being is determined by his pains and pleasures; and that his happiness corresponds with the degree in which his pleasures are great, and his pains are small.

Human pains and pleasures are derived from two sources:—They are produced, either by our fellow-men, or by causes independent of other men.

We may assume it as another principle, that the concern of Government is with the former of these two sources; that its business is to increase to the utmost the pleasures, and diminish to the utmost the pains, which men derive from one another.

Of the laws of nature, on which the condition of man depends, that which is attended with the greatest number of consequences, is the necessity of labour for obtaining the means of subsistence, as well as the means of the greatest part of our pleasures. This is, no doubt, the primary cause of Government; for, if nature had produced spontaneously all the objects which we desire, and in sufficient abundance for the desires of all, there would have been no source of dispute or of injury among men; nor would any man have possessed the means of ever acquiring authority over another.

The results are exceedingly different, when nature produces the objects of desire not in sufficient abundance for all. The source of dispute is then exhaustless; and every man has the means of acquiring authority over others, in proportion to the quantity of those objects which he is able to possess.

In this case, the end to be obtained, through Government as the means, is, to make that distribution of the scanty materials of happiness, which would insure the greatest sum of it in the members of the community, taken altogether, preventing every individual, or combination of individuals, from interfering with that distribution, or making any man to have less than his share.

When it is considered that most of the objects of desire, and even the means of subsistence, are the product of labour, it is evident that the means of insuring labour must be provided for as the foundation of all.

The means for the insuring of labour are of two sorts; the one made out of the matter of evil, the other made out of the matter of good.

The first sort is commonly denominated force; and, under its application, the labourers are slaves. This mode of procuring labour we need not consider; for, if the end of Government be to produce the greatest happiness of the greatest number, that end cannot be attained by making the greatest number slaves.

The other mode of obtaining labour is by allurement, or the advantage which it brings. To obtain all the objects of desire in the greatest possible quantity, we must obtain labour in the greatest possible quantity; and, to obtain labour in the greatest possible quantity, we must raise to the greatest possible height the advantage attached to labour. It is impossible to attach to labour a greater degree of advantage than the whole of the product of labour. Why so? Because, if you give more to one man than the produce of his labour, you can do so only by taking it away from the produce of some other man's labour. The greatest possible happiness of society is, therefore, attained by insuring to every man the greatest possible quantity of the produce of his labour.

How is this to be accomplished? for it is obvious that every man, who has not all the objects of his desire, has inducement to take them from any other man who is weaker than himself: and how is he to be prevented?

One mode is sufficiently obvious; and it does not appear that there is any other: The union of a certain number of men, to protect one another. The object, it is plain, can best be attained when a great number of men combine, and delegate to a small number the power necessary for protecting them all. This is Government.

With respect to the end of Government, or that for the sake of which it exists, it is not conceived to be necessary, on the present occasion, that the analysis should be carried any further. What follows is an attempt to analyze the means.

II

The Means of attaining the End of Government;
viz. Power, and Securities against the
Abuse of that Power

Two things are here to be considered; the power with which the small number are entrusted; and the use which they are to make of it.

With respect to the first, there is no difficulty. The elements, out of which the power of coercing others is fabricated, are obvious to all. Of these we shall, therefore, not lengthen this article by any explanation.

All the difficult questions of Government relate to the means of restraining those, in whose hands are lodged the powers necessary for the protection of all, from making a bad use of it.

Whatever would be the temptations under which individuals would lie, if there was no Government, to take the objects of desire from others weaker than themselves, under the same temptations the members of Government lie, to take the objects of desire from the members of the community, if they are not prevented from doing so. Whatever, then, are the reasons for establishing Government, the very same exactly are

6

the reasons for establishing securities, that those entrusted with the powers necessary for protecting others make use of them for that purpose solely, and not for the purpose of taking from the members of the community the objects of desire.

III

That the requisite Securities against the Abuse of Power, are not found in any of the simple Forms of Government

There are three modes in which it may be supposed that the powers for the protection of the community are capable of being exercised. The community may undertake the protection of itself, and of its members. The powers of protection may be placed in the hands of a few. And, lastly, they may be placed in the hands of an individual. The Many, The Few, The One; These varieties appear to exhaust the subject. It is not possible to conceive any hands, or combination of hands, in which the powers of protection can be lodged, which will not fall under one or other of those descriptions. And these varieties correspond to the three forms of Government, the Democratical, the Aristocratical, and the Monarchical.

It will be necessary to look somewhat closely at each of these forms in their order.

1. THE DEMOCRATICAL.—It is obviously impossible that the community in a body can be present to afford protection to each of its members. It must employ individuals for that purpose. Em-

ploying individuals, it must choose them; it must lay down the rules under which they are to act; and it must punish them, if they act in disconformity to those rules. In these functions are included the three great operations of Government —Administration, Legislation, and Judicature. The community, to perform any of these operations, must be assembled. This circumstance alone seems to form a conclusive objection against the democratical form. To assemble the whole of a community as often as the business of Government requires performance would almost preclude the existence of labour; hence that of property; and hence the existence of the community itself.

There is another objection, not less conclusive. A whole community would form a numerous assembly. But all numerous assemblies are essentially incapable of business. It is unnecessary to be tedious in the proof of this proposition. In an assembly, every thing must be done by speaking and assenting. But where the assembly is numerous, so many persons desire to speak, and feelings, by mutual inflammation, become so violent, that calm and effectual deliberation is impossible.

It may be taken, therefore, as a position, from which there will be no dissent, that a community in mass is ill adapted for the business of Government. There is no principle more in conformity

9

with the sentiments and the practice of the people than this. The management of the joint affairs of any considerable body of the people they never undertake for themselves. What they uniformly do is, to choose a certain number of themselves to be the actors in their stead. Even in the case of a common Benefit Club, the members choose a Committee of Management, and content themselves with a general controul.

2. THE ARISTOCRATICAL.—This term applies to all those cases, in which the powers of Government are held by any number of persons intermediate between a single person and the majority. When the number is small, it is common to call the Government an Oligarchy; when it is considerable, to call it an Aristocracy. The cases are essentially the same; because the motives which operate in both are the same. This is a proposition which carries, we think, its own evidence along with it. We, therefore, assume it as a point which will not be disputed.

The source of evil is radically different, in the case of Aristocracy, from what it is in that of Democracy.

The Community cannot have an interest opposite to its interest. To affirm this would be a contradiction in terms. The Community within itself, and with respect to itself, can have no sinister interest. One Community may intend the

evil of another; never its own. This is an indubitable proposition, and one of great importance.
The Community may act wrong from mistake.
To suppose that it could from design, would be to
suppose that human beings can wish their own
misery.

The circumstances, from which the inaptitude
of the community, as a body, for the business of
Government, arises, namely, the inconvenience
of assembling them, and the inconvenience of
their numbers when assembled, do not necessarily
exist in the case of Aristocracy. If the number of
those who hold among them the powers of
Government is so great, as to make it inconvenient
to assemble them, or impossible for them to de-
liberate calmly when assembled, this is only an
objection to so extended an Aristocracy, and has
no application to an Aristocracy not too numerous, when assembled, for the best exercise of deliberation.

The question is, whether such an Aristocracy
may be trusted to make that use of the powers of
Government which is most conducive to the end
for which Government exists?

There may be a strong presumption that any
Aristocracy, monopolizing the powers of Government, would not possess intellectual powers in any
very high perfection. Intellectual powers are the
offspring of labour. But an hereditary Aristocracy

are deprived of the strongest motives to labour. The greater part of them will, therefore, be defective in those mental powers. This is one objection, and an important one, though not the greatest.

We have already observed, that the reason for which Government exists is, that one man, if stronger than another, will take from him whatever that other possesses and he desires. But if one man will do this, so will several. And if powers are put into the hands of a comparatively small number, called an Aristocracy, powers which make them stronger than the rest of the community, they will take from the rest of the community as much as they please of the objects of desire. They will, thus, defeat the very end for which Government was instituted. The unfitness, therefore, of an Aristocracy to be entrusted with the powers of Government, rests on demonstration.

3. THE MONARCHICAL.—It will be seen, and therefore words to make it manifest are unnecessary, that, in most respects, the Monarchical form of Government agrees with the Aristocratical, and is liable to the same objections.

If Government is founded upon this, as a law of human nature, that a man, if able, will take from others any thing which they have and he desires, it is sufficiently evident that when a man is called a King, it does not change his nature; so that when he has got power to enable him to take from every man what he pleases, he will take whatever he pleases. To suppose that he will not, is to affirm that Government is unnecessary; and that human beings will abstain from injuring one another of their own accord.

It is very evident that this reasoning extends to every modification of the smaller number. Whenever the powers of Government are placed in any hands other than those of the community, whether those of one man, of a few, or of several, those principles of human nature which imply that Government is at all necessary, imply that those persons will make use of them to defeat the very end for which Government exists.

IV

An Objection stated—and answered

One observation, however, suggests itself. Allowing, it may be said, that this deduction is perfect, and the inference founded upon it indisputable, it is yet true, that if there were no Government, every man would be exposed to depredation from every man; but, under an Aristocracy, he is exposed to it only from a few; under a Monarchy, only from one.

This is a highly-important objection, and deserves to be minutely investigated.

It is sufficiently obvious, that, if every man is liable to be deprived of what he possesses at the will of every man stronger than himself, the existence of property is impossible; and, if the existence of property is impossible, so also is that of labour, of the means of subsistence for an enlarged community, and hence of the community itself. If the members of such a community are liable to deprivation by only a few hundred men, the members of an Aristocracy, it may not be impossible to satiate that limited number with a limited portion of the objects belonging to all. Allowing this view of the subject to be correct, it follows, that the smaller the number of hands into which the powers of Government are permitted to pass, the happier it will be for the community: that an Oligarchy, therefore, is better than an Aristocracy, and a Monarchy better than either.

This view of the subject deserves to be the more carefully considered, because the conclusion to which it leads is the same with that which has been adopted and promulgated, by some of the most profound and most benevolent investigators of human affairs. That Government by one man, altogether unlimited and uncontrolled, is better than Government by any modification of Aristocracy, is the celebrated opinion of Mr Hobbes, and of the French *Economists*, supported on reasonings which it is not easy to controvert. Government by the many, they with reason considered an impossibility. They inferred, therefore, that, of all the possible forms of Government, absolute Monarchy is the best.

Experience, if we look only at the outside of the facts, appears to be divided on this subject. Absolute Monarchy, under Neros and Caligulas, under such men as Emperors of Morocco and Sultans of Turkey, is the scourge of human nature. On the other side, the people of Denmark, tired out with the oppression of an Aristocracy, resolved that their King should be absolute; and, under their absolute Monarch, are as well governed as any people in Europe. In Greece, notwithstanding the defects of Democracy, human nature ran a more brilliant career than it has ever done in any other age or country.

As the surface of history affords, therefore, no certain principle of decision, we must go beyond the surface, and penetrate to the springs within.

When it is said that one man, or a limited number of men, will soon be satiated with the objects of desire, and, when they have taken from the community what suffices to satiate them, will protect its members in the enjoyment of the remainder, an important element of the calculation is left out. Human beings are not a passive substance. If human beings, in respect to their rulers, were the same as sheep in respect to their shepherd; and if the King, or the Aristocracy, were as totally exempt from all fear of resistance from the people, and all chance of obtaining more obedience from severity, as the shepherd in the case of the sheep, it does appear that there would be a limit to the motive for taking to one's self the objects of desire. The case will be found to be very much altered when the idea is taken into the account, first, of the resistance to his will which one human being may expect from another; and secondly, of that perfection in obedience which fear alone can produce.

That one human being will desire to render the person and property of another subservient to his pleasures, notwithstanding the pain or loss of pleasure which it may occasion to that other individual, is the foundation of Government. The desire of the object implies the desire of the power necessary to accomplish the object. The desire, therefore, of that power which is necessary to render the persons and properties of human beings subservient to our pleasures, is a grand governing law of human nature.

What is implied in that desire of power; and what is the extent to which it carries the actions of men; are the questions which it is necessary to resolve, in order to discover the limit which nature has set to the desire on the part of a King, or an Aristocracy, to inflict evil upon the community for their own advantage.

Power is a means to an end. The end is every thing, without exception, which the human being calls pleasure, and the removal of pain. The grand instrument for attaining what a man likes is the actions of other men. Power, in its most appropriate signification, therefore, means security for the conformity between the will of one man and the acts of other men. This, we presume, is not a proposition which will be disputed. The master has power over his servant, because when he wills him to do so and so—in other words,

expresses a desire that he would do so and so, he
possesses a kind of security that the actions of the
man will correspond to his desire. The General
commands his soldiers to perform certain operations, the King commands his subjects to act in
a certain manner, and their power is complete or
not complete, in proportion as the conformity is
complete or not complete between the actions
willed and the actions performed. The actions of
other men, considered as means for the attain-
ment of the objects of our desire, are perfect or
imperfect, in proportion as they are or are not
certainly and invariably correspondent to our
will. There is no limit, therefore, to the demand of
security for the perfection of that correspondence.
A man is never satisfied with a smaller degree if
he can obtain a greater. And as there is no man
whatsoever, whose acts, in some degree or other,
in some way or other, more immediately or more
remotely, may not have some influence as means
to our ends, there is no man, the conformity of
whose acts to our will we would not give something to secure. The demand, therefore, of power
over the acts of other men is really boundless. It
is boundless in two ways; boundless in the number
of persons to whom we would extend it, and
boundless in its degree over the actions of each.

It would be nugatory to say, with a view to ex-
plain away this important principle, that some

human beings may be so remotely connected with our interests as to make the desire of a conformity between our will and their actions evanescent. It is quite enough to assume, what nobody will deny, that our desire of that conformity is unlimited, in respect to all those men whose actions can be supposed to have any influence on our pains and pleasures. With respect to the rulers of a community, this at least is certain, that they have a desire for the uniformity between their will and the actions of every man in the community. And for our present purpose, this is as wide a field as we need to embrace.

With respect to the community, then, we deem it an established truth, that the rulers, one or a few, desire an exact conformity between their will and the acts of every member of the community. It remains for us to inquire to what description of acts it is the nature of this desire to give existence.

There are two classes of means by which the conformity between the will of one man and the acts of other men may be accomplished. The one is pleasure, the other pain.

With regard to securities of the pleasurable sort for obtaining a conformity between one man's will and the acts of other men, it is evident, from experience, that when a man possesses a command over the objects of desire, he may, by imparting those objects to other men, insure, to a great extent, conformity between his will and their actions. It follows, and is also matter of experience, that the greater the quantity of the objects of desire, which he may thus impart to other men, the greater is the number of men between whose actions and his own will he can insure a conformity. As it has been demonstrated that there is no limit to the number of men whose actions we desire to have conformable to our will, it follows, with equal evidence, that there is no limit to the command which we desire to possess over the objects which ensure this result.

It is, therefore, not true, that there is in the mind of a King, or in the minds of an Aristocracy, any point of saturation with the objects of desire. The opinion, in examination of which we have gone through the preceding analysis, that a King or an Aristocracy may be satiated with the objects of desire, and, after being satiated, leave to the members of the community the greater part of what belongs to them, is an opinion founded upon a partial and incomplete view of the laws of human nature.

We have next to consider the securities of the painful sort which may be employed for attaining conformity between the acts of one man and the will of another.

We are of opinion, that the importance of this part of the subject has not been duly considered;

and that the business of Government will be ill understood, till its numerous consequences have been fully developed.

Pleasure appears to be a feeble instrument of obedience in comparison with pain. It is much more easy to despise pleasure than pain. Above all, it is important to consider, that in this class of instruments is included the power of taking away life, and with it of taking away not only all the pleasures of reality, but, what goes so far beyond them, all the pleasures of hope. This class of securities is, therefore, incomparably the strongest. He who desires obedience, to a high degree of exactness, cannot be satisfied with the power of giving pleasure, he must have the power of inflicting pain. He who desires it, to the highest possible degree of exactness, must desire power of inflicting pain sufficient at least to insure that degree of exactness; that is, an unlimited power of inflicting pain; for, as there is no possible mark by which to distinguish what is sufficient and what is not, and as the human mind sets no bounds to its avidity for the securities of what it deems eminently good, it is sure to extend, beyond almost any limits, its desire of the power of giving pain to others.

It may, however, be said, that how inseparable a part soever of human nature it may appear to be, to desire to possess unlimited power of inflicting pain upon others, it does not follow, that those who possess it will have a desire to make use of it.

This is the next part of the inquiry upon which we have to enter; and we need not add that it merits all the attention of those who would possess correct ideas upon a subject which involves the greatest interests of mankind.

The chain of inference, in this case, is close and strong, to a most unusual degree. A man desires that the actions of other men shall be instantly and accurately correspondent to his will. He desires that the actions of the greatest possible number shall be so. Terror is the grand instrument. Terror can work only through assurance that evil will follow any want of conformity between the will and the actions willed. Every failure must, therefore, be punished. As there are no bounds to the mind's desire of its pleasure, there are of course no bounds to its desire of perfection in the instruments of that pleasure. There are, therefore, no bounds to its desire of exactness in the conformity between its will and the actions willed; and, by consequence, to the strength of that terror which is its procuring cause. Every, the most minute, failure, must be visited with the heaviest infliction: and, as failure in extreme exactness must frequently happen, the occasions of cruelty must be incessant.

We have thus arrived at several conclusions of the highest possible importance. We have seen, that the very principle of human nature upon which the necessity of Government is founded, the propensity of one man to possess himself of the objects of desire at the cost of another, leads on, by infallible sequence, where power over a community is attained, and nothing checks, not only to that degree of plunder which leaves the members (excepting always the recipients and instruments of the plunder) the bare means of subsistence, but to that degree of cruelty which is necessary to keep in existence the most intense terror.

The world affords some decisive experiments upon human nature, in exact conformity with these conclusions. An English Gentleman may be taken as a favourable specimen of civilization, of knowledge, of humanity, of all the qualities, in short, that make human nature estimable. The degree in which he desires to possess power over his fellow-creatures, and the degree of oppression to which he finds motives for carrying the exercise of that power, will afford a standard from which, assuredly, there can be no appeal. Wherever the same motives exist, the same conduct, as that displayed by the English Gentleman, may be expected to follow, in all men not farther advanced in human excellence than him. In the West

Indies, before that vigilant attention of the English nation, which now, for thirty years, has imposed so great a check upon the masters of slaves, there was not a perfect absence of all check upon the dreadful propensities of power. But yet it is true, that these propensities led English Gentlemen, not only to deprive their slaves of property, and to make property of their fellow-creatures, but to treat them with a degree of cruelty, the very description of which froze the blood of their countrymen, who were placed in less unfavourable circumstances. The motives of this deplorable conduct are exactly those which we have described above, as arising out of the universal desire to render the actions of other men exactly conformable to our will. It is of great importance to remark, that not one item in the motives which had led English Gentlemen to make slaves of their fellow-creatures, and to reduce them to the very worst condition in which the negroes have been found in the West Indies, can be shown to be wanting, or to be less strong in the set of motives, which universally operate upon the men who have power over their fellow-creatures. It is proved, therefore, by the closest deduction from the acknowledged laws of human nature, and by direct and decisive experiments, that the ruling One, or the ruling Few, would, if checks did not operate in the way of prevention, reduce the great mass of the people subject to their power, at least to the condition of negroes in the West Indies.*

We have thus seen, that of the forms of Government, which have been called the three simple forms, not one is adequate to the ends which Government is appointed to secure; that the community itself, which alone is free from motives opposite to those ends, is incapacitated by its numbers from performing the business of Government; and that whether Government is intrusted to one or a few, they have not only motives opposite to those ends, but motives which will carry them, if unchecked, to inflict the greatest evils.

These conclusions are so conformable to ordinary conceptions, that it would hardly have been necessary, if the development had not been of importance for some of our subsequent investigations, to have taken any pains with the proof of them. In this country, at least, it will be remarked, in conformity with so many writers, that the imperfection of the three simple forms of Government is apparent; that the ends of Government can be attained in perfection only, as under the British Constitution, by an union of all the three.

* An acute sense of this important truth is expressed by the President Montesquieu: "C'est une expérience éternelle, que tout homme qui a du pouvoir est porté à en abuser; il va jusqu'à ce qu'il trouve de limites."—*Esp. de Lois*, II. 4.

V

*That the requisite Securities are not found in a
Union of the Three simple Forms of Government;
—Doctrine of the Constitutional Balance*

The doctrine of the union of the three simple
forms of Government is the next part of this important subject which we are called upon to
examine.

The first thing which it is obvious to remark
upon it, is, that it has been customary, in regard
to this part of the inquiry, to beg the question. The
good effects which have been ascribed to the union
of the three simple forms of Government, have
been *supposed*; and the supposition has commonly
been allowed. No proof has been adduced; or if
any thing have the appearance of proof, it has
only been a reference to the British Constitution.
The British Constitution, it has been said, is an
union of the three simple forms of Government;
and the British Government is excellent. To render the instance of the British Government in any
degree a proof of the doctrine in question, it is
evident that three points must be established; 1st,
That the British Government is not in show, but in
substance, an union of the three simple forms;

2dly, That it has peculiar excellence; and, 3dly, That its excellence arises from the union so supposed, and not from any other cause. As these points have always been taken for granted without examination, the question with respect to the effects of an union of the three simple forms of Government may be considered as yet unsolved.

The positions which we have already established with regard to human nature, and which we assume as foundations, are these: That the actions of men are governed by their wills, and their wills by their desires: That their desires are directed to pleasure and relief from pain as *ends*, and to wealth and power as the principal means: That to the desire of these means there is no limit; and that the actions which flow from this unlimited desire are the constituents whereof bad Government is made. Reasoning correctly from these acknowledged laws of human nature, we shall presently discover what opinion, with respect to the mixture of the different species of Government, it will be incumbent upon us to adopt.

The theory in question implies, that of the powers of Government, one portion is held by the King, one by the Aristocracy, and one by the people. It also implies, that there is on the part of each of them a certain unity of will, otherwise they would not act as three separate powers. This being understood, we proceed to the inquiry.

From the principles which we have already laid down, it follows, That of the objects of human desire—and, speaking more definitely, of the means to the ends of human desire, namely, wealth and power—each of the three parties will endeavour to obtain as much as possible.

After what has been said, it is not suspected that any reader will deny this proposition; but it is of importance that he keep in his mind a very clear conception of it.

If any expedient presents itself to any of the supposed parties, effectual to said end, and not opposed to any preferred object of pursuit, we may infer, with certainty, that it will be adopted. One effectual expedient is not more effectual than obvious. Any two of the parties, by combining, may swallow up the third. That such combination will take place, appears to be as certain as any thing which depends upon human will; because there are strong motives in favour of it, and none that can be conceived in opposition to it. Whether the portions of power, as originally distributed to the parties, be supposed to be equal or unequal, the mixture of three of the kinds of Government, it is thus evident, cannot possibly exist.

This proposition appears to be so perfectly proved, that we do not think it necessary to dwell here upon the subject. As a part, however, of this doctrine, of the mixture of the simple forms of

Government, it may be proper to inquire, whether an union may not be possible of two of them.

Three varieties of this union may be conceived; the union of the Monarchy with Aristocracy, or the union of either with Democracy.

Let us first suppose that Monarchy is united with Aristocracy. Their power is equal or not equal. If it is not equal, it follows, as a necessary consequence, from the principles which we have already established, that the stronger will take from the weaker, till it engrosses the whole. The only question, therefore, is, What will happen when the power is equal?

In the first place, it seems impossible that such equality should ever exist. How is it to be established? Or by what criterion is it to be ascertained? If there is no such criterion, it must, in all cases, be the result of chance. If so, the chances against it are as infinite to one. The idea, therefore, is wholly chimerical and absurd.

Besides, A disposition to overrate one's own advantages, and underrate those of other men, is a known law of human nature. Suppose, what would be little less than miraculous, that equality were established, this propensity would lead each of the parties to conceive itself the strongest. The consequence would be that they would go to war, and contend till one or other was subdued. Either

29

those laws of human nature, upon which all reasoning with respect to Government proceeds, must be denied, and then the utility of Government itself may be denied, or this conclusion is demonstrated. Again, if this equality were established, is there a human being who can suppose that it would last? If any thing be known about human affairs it is this, that they are in perpetual change. If nothing else interfered, the difference of men in respect of talents, would abundantly produce the effect. Suppose your equality to be established at the time when your King is a man of talents, and suppose his successor to be the reverse; your equality no longer exists. The moment one of the parties is superior, it begins to profit by its superiority, and the inequality is daily increased. It is unnecessary to extend the investigation to the remaining cases, the union of democracy with either of the other two kinds of Government. It is very evident that the same reasoning would lead to the same results.

In this doctrine of the mixture of the simple forms of Government, is included the celebrated theory of the Balance among the component parts of a Government. By this, it is supposed, that, when a Government is composed of Monarchy, Aristocracy, and Democracy, they balance one another, and by mutual checks produce good government. A few words will suffice to show, that, if any theory deserve the epithets of "wild, visionary, chimerical", it is that of the Balance. If there are three powers, how is it possible to prevent two of them from combining to swallow up the third?

The analysis which we have already performed, will enable us to trace rapidly the concatenation of causes and effects in this imagined case.

We have already seen that the interest of the community, considered in the aggregate, or in the democratical point of view, is, that each individual should receive protection, and that the powers which are constituted for that purpose should be employed exclusively for that purpose. As this is a proposition wholly indisputable, it is also one to which all correct reasoning upon matters of Government must have a perpetual reference.

We have also seen that the interest of the King, and of the governing Aristocracy, is directly the reverse; it is to have unlimited power over the rest of the community, and to use it for their own advantage. In the supposed case of the balance of the Monarchical, Aristocratical, and Democratical powers, it cannot be for the interest of either the Monarchy or the Aristocracy to combine with the Democracy; because it is the interest of the Democracy, or community at large, that neither the King nor the Aristocracy should have one particle of power, or one particle of the wealth of the community, for their own advantage.

The Democracy or Community have all possible motives to endeavour to prevent the Monarchy and Aristocracy from exercising power, or obtaining the wealth of the community, for their own advantage: The Monarchy and Aristocracy have all possible motives for endeavouring to obtain unlimited power over the persons and property of the community: The consequence is inevitable; they have all possible motives for combining to obtain that power, and unless the people have power enough to be a match for both, they have no protection. The balance, therefore, is a thing, the existence of which, upon the best possible evidence, is to be regarded as impossible. The appearances which have given colour to the supposition are altogether delusive.

VI

In the Representative System alone the Securities for good Government are to be found

What then is to be done? For, according to this reasoning, we may be told that good Government appears to be impossible. The people, as a body, cannot perform the business of Government for themselves. If the powers of Government are entrusted to one man, or a few men, and a Monarchy, or governing Aristocracy, is formed, the results are fatal: And it appears that a combination of the simple forms is impossible.

Notwithstanding the truth of these propositions, it is not yet proved that good Government is impossible. For though the people, who cannot exercise the powers of Government themselves, must entrust them to some one individual or set of individuals, and such individuals will infallibly have the strongest motives to make a bad use of them, it is possible that checks may be found sufficient to prevent them. The next subject of inquiry, then, is the doctrine of checks. It is sufficiently conformable to the established and fashionable opinions to say, that, upon the right constitution of checks, all goodness of Government depends. To this proposition we fully subscribe. Nothing, therefore, can exceed the importance of correct conclusions upon this subject. After the developements already made, it is hoped that the inquiry will be neither intricate nor unsatisfactory.

In the grand discovery of modern times, the system of representation, the solution of all the difficulties, both speculative and practical, will perhaps be found. If it cannot, we seem to be forced upon the extraordinary conclusion, that good Government is impossible. For as there is no individual, or combination of individuals, except the community itself, who would not have an interest in bad Government, if entrusted with its powers; and as the community itself is incapable of exercising those powers, and must entrust them to some individual or combination of individuals, the conclusion is obvious: The Community itself must check those individuals, else they will follow their interest, and produce bad Government.

But how is it the Community can check? The community can act only when assembled: And then it is incapable of acting.

The community, however, can chuse Representatives: And the question is, whether the Representatives of the Community can operate as a check?

VII

What is required in a Representative Body to make it a Security for good Government?

We may begin by laying down two propositions, which appear to involve a great portion of the inquiry; and about which it is unlikely that there will be any dispute.

I. The checking body must have a degree of power sufficient for the business of checking.

II. It must have an identity of interest with the community; otherwise it will make a mischievous use of its power.

I. To measure the degree of power which is requisite upon any occasion, we must consider the degree of power which is necessary to be overcome. Just as much as suffices for that purpose is requisite, and no more. We have then to inquire what power it is which the Representatives of the community, acting as a check, need power to overcome. The answer here is easily given. It is all that power, wheresoever lodged, which they, in whose hands it is lodged, have an interest in misusing. We have already seen, that to whomsoever the community entrusts the powers of Government, whether one, or a few, they have an

3–2

interest in misusing them. All the power, therefore, which the one or the few, or which the one and the few combined, can apply to insure the accomplishment of their sinister ends, the checking body must have power to overcome, otherwise its check will be unavailing. In other words, there will be no check.

This is so exceedingly evident, that we hardly think it necessary to say another word in illustration of it. If a King is prompted by the inherent principles of human nature to seek the gratification of his will; and if he finds an obstacle in that pursuit, he removes it, of course, if he can. If any man, or any set of men, oppose him, he overcomes them, if he is able; and to prevent him, they must, at the least, have equal power with himself.

The same is the case with an Aristocracy. To oppose them with success in pursuing their interest at the expense of the community, the checking body must have power successfully to resist whatever power they possess. If there is both a King and an Aristocracy, and if they would combine to put down the checking force, and to pursue their mutual interest at the expense of the community, the checking body must have sufficient power successfully to resist the united power of both King and Aristocracy.

These conclusions are not only indisputable, but the very theory of the British Constitution is erected upon them. The House of Commons, according to that theory, is the checking body. It is also an admitted doctrine, that if the King had the power of bearing down any opposition to his will that could be made by the House of Commons; or if the King and the House of Lords combined had the power of bearing down its opposition to their joint will, it would cease to have the power of checking them; it must, therefore, have a power sufficient to overcome the united power of both.

II. All the questions which relate to the degree of power necessary to be given to that checking body, on the perfection of whose operations all the goodness of Government depends, are thus pretty easily solved. The grand difficulty consists in finding the means of constituting a checking body, whose powers shall not be turned against the community for whose protection it is created.

There can be no doubt, that if power is granted to a body of men, called Representatives, they, like any other men, will use their power, not for the advantage of the community, but for their own advantage, if they can. The only question is, therefore, how they can be prevented? in other words, how are the interests of the Representatives to be identified with those of the community?

Each Representative may be considered in two capacities; in his capacity of Representative, in

37

which he has the exercise of power over others, and in his capacity of Member of the Community, in which others have the exercise of power over him.

If things were so arranged, that, in his capacity of Representative, it would be impossible for him to do himself so much good by misgovernment, as he would do himself harm in his capacity of member of the community, the object would be accomplished. We have already seen, that the amount of power assigned to the checking body cannot be diminished beyond a certain amount. It must be sufficient to overcome all resistance on the part of all those in whose hands the powers of Government are lodged. But if the power assigned to the Representative cannot be diminished in amount, there is only one other way in which it can be diminished, and that is, in duration.

This, then, is the instrument; lessening of duration is the instrument, by which, if by any thing, the object is to be attained. The smaller the period of time during which any man retains his capacity of Representative, as compared with the time in which he is simply a member of the community, the more difficult it will be to compensate the sacrifice of the interests of the longer period, by the profits of misgovernment during the shorter.

This is an old and approved method of identifying as nearly as possible the interests of those who rule with the interests of those who are ruled. It is in pursuance of this advantage, that the Members of the British House of Commons have always been chosen for a limited period. If the Members were hereditary, or even if they were chosen for life, every inquirer would immediately pronounce that they would employ, for their own advantage, the powers entrusted to them; and that they would go just as far in abusing the persons and properties of the people, as their estimate of the powers and spirit of the people to resist them would allow them to contemplate as safe.

As it thus appears, by the consent of all men, from the time when the Romans made their Consuls annual, down to the present day, that the end is to be attained by limiting the duration, either of the acting, or (which is better) of the checking power, the next question is, to what degree should the limitation proceed?

The general answer is plain. It should proceed, till met by overbalancing inconveniences on the other side. What then are the inconveniences which are likely to flow from a too limited duration?

They are of two sorts; those which affect the performance of the service, for which the individuals are chosen, and those which arise from the trouble of election. It is sufficiently obvious, that the business of Government requires time to perform it. The matter must be proposed, deliberated upon, a resolution must be taken, and executed. If the powers of Government were to be shifted from one set of hands to another every day, the business of Government could not proceed. Two conclusions, then, we may adopt with perfect certainty; that whatsoever time is necessary to perform the periodical round of the stated operations of Government, this should be allotted to those who are invested with the checking powers; and secondly, that no time, which is not necessary for that purpose, should by any means be allotted to them. With respect to the inconvenience arising from frequency of election, though, it is evident, that the trouble of election, which is always something, should not be repeated oftener than is necessary, no great allowance will need to be made for it, because it may easily be reduced to an inconsiderable amount.

As it thus appears, that limiting the duration of their power is a security against the sinister interest of the people's Representatives, so it appears that it is the only security of which the nature of the case admits. The only other means which could be employed to that end, would be punishment on account of abuse. It is easy, however, to see, that punishment could not be effectually applied. In order for punishment, definition is required of the punishable acts; and proof must be established of the commission. But abuses of power may be carried to a great extent, without allowing the means of proving a determinate offence. No part of political experience is more perfect than this.

If the limiting of duration be the only security, it is unnecessary to speak of the importance which ought to be attached to it.

In the principle of limiting the duration of the power delegated to the Representatives of the people, is not included the idea of changing them. The same individual may be chosen any number of times. The check of the short period, for which he is chosen, and during which he can promote his sinister interest, is the same upon the man who has been chosen and re-chosen twenty times, as upon the man who has been chosen for the first time. And there is good reason for always re-electing the man who has done his duty, because the longer he serves, the better acquainted he becomes with the business of the service. Upon this principle of rechoosing, or of the permanency of the individual, united with the power of change, has been recommended the plan of permanent service with perpetual power of removal. This, it has been said, reduces the period within which the Representative can promote his sinister interest to the narrowest possible limits; because the moment when his Constituents begin to suspect him, that moment they may turn him out. On the other hand, if he continues faithful, the trouble of election is performed once for all, and the man serves as long as he lives. Some disadvantages, on the other hand, would accompany this plan. The present, however, is not the occasion on which the balance of different plans is capable of being compared.

VIII

What is required in the Elective Body to secure the requisite Properties in the Representative Body

Having considered the means which are capable of being employed for identifying the interest of the Representatives, when chosen, with that of the persons who choose them, it remains that we endeavour to bring to view the principles which ought to guide in determining who the persons are by whom the act of choosing ought to be performed.

It is most evident, that, upon this question, every thing depends. It can be of no consequence to insure, by shortness of duration, a conformity between the conduct of the Representatives and the will of those who appoint them, if those who appoint them have an interest opposite to that of the community; because those who choose will, according to the principles of human nature, make choice of such persons as will act according to their wishes. As this is a direct inference from the very principle on which Government itself is founded, we assume it as indisputable.

We have seen already, that if one man has power over others placed in his hands, he will make use of it for an evil purpose; for the purpose of rendering those other men the abject instruments of his will. If we, then, suppose, that one man has the power of choosing the Representatives of the people, it follows, that he will choose men who will use their power as Representatives for the promotion of this his sinister interest.

We have likewise seen, that when a few men have power given them over others, they will make use of it exactly for the same ends, and to the same extent, as the one man. It equally follows, that, if a small number of men have the choice of the Representatives, such Representatives will be chosen as will promote the interests of that small number, by reducing, if possible, the rest of the community to be the abject and helpless slaves of their will.

In all these cases, it is obvious and indisputable, that all the benefits of the Representative system are lost. The Representative system is, in that case, only an operose and clumsy machinery for doing that which might as well be done without it; reducing the community to subjection, under the One, or the Few.

When we say the Few, it is seen that, in this case, it is of no importance whether we mean a few hundreds, or a few thousands, or even many thousands. The operation of the sinister interest is the same; and the fate is the same of all that part of the community over whom the power is exercised. A numerous Aristocracy has never been found to be less oppressive than an Aristocracy confined to a few.

The general conclusion, therefore, which is evidently established is this; that the benefits of the Representative system are lost, in all cases in which the interests of the choosing body are not the same with those of the community.

It is very evident, that if the community itself were the choosing body, the interest of the community and that of the choosing body would be the same. The question is, whether that of any portion of the community, if erected into the choosing body, would remain the same?

One thing is pretty clear, that all those individuals whose interests are indisputably included in those of other individuals, may be struck off without inconvenience. In this light may be viewed all children, up to a certain age, whose interests are involved in those of their parents. In this light, also, women may be regarded, the interest of almost all of whom is involved either in that of their fathers or in that of their husbands.

Having ascertained that an interest identical with that of the whole community, is to be found in the aggregate males, of an age to be regarded as *sui juris*, who may be regarded as the natural Representatives of the whole population, we have to go on, and inquire, whether this requisite quality may not be found in some less number, some aliquot part of that body.

As degrees of mental qualities are not easily ascertained, outward and visible signs must be taken to distinguish, for this purpose, one part of these males from another. Applicable signs of this description appear to be three; Years, Property, Profession or Mode of Life.

According to the first of these means of distinction, a portion of the males, to any degree limited, may be taken, by prescribing an advanced period of life at which the power of voting for a Representative should commence. According to the second, the elective body may be limited, by allowing a vote to those only who possess a certain amount of property or of income. According to the third, they may be limited, by allowing a vote only to such persons as belong to certain professions, or certain connexions and interests. What we have to inquire is, if the interest of the number, limited and set apart, upon any of those principles, as the organ of choice for a body of Representatives, will be the same with the interest of the community?

With respect to the first principle of selection, that of age, it would appear that a considerable latitude may be taken without inconvenience. Suppose the age of forty were prescribed, as that at which the right of Suffrage should commence; scarcely any laws could be made for the benefit of all the men of forty which would not be laws for the benefit of all the rest of the community.

The great principle of security here is, that the men of forty have a deep interest in the welfare of the younger men; for otherwise it might be objected, with perfect truth, that, if decisive power were placed in the hands of men of forty years of age, they would have an interest, just as any other detached portion of the community, in pursuing that career which we have already described, for reducing the rest of the community to the state of abject slaves. But the great majority of old men have sons, whose interest they regard as an essential part of their own. This is a law of human nature. There is, therefore, no great danger that, in such an arrangement as this, the interests of the young would be greatly sacrificed to those of the old.

We come next to the inquiry, whether the interest of a body of electors, constituted by the possession of a certain amount of property or income, would be the same with the interest of the community?

It will not be disputed, that, if the qualification were raised so high that only a few hundreds possessed it, the case would be exactly the same with that of the consignment of the Electoral Suffrage to an Aristocracy. This we have already considered, and have seen that it differs in form rather than substance from a simple Aristocracy. We have likewise seen, that it alters not the case in regard to the community, whether the Aristocracy be some hundreds or many thousands. One thing is, therefore, completely ascertained, that a pecuniary qualification, unless it were very low, would only create an Aristocratical Government, and produce all the evils which we have shown to belong to that organ of misrule.

This question, however, deserves to be a little more minutely considered. Let us next take the opposite extreme. Let us suppose that the qualification is very low, so low as to include the great majority of the people. It would not be easy for the people who have very little property, to separate their interests from those of the people who have none. It is not the interest of those who have little property to give undue advantages to the possession of property, which those who have the great portions of it would turn against themselves.

It may, therefore, be said, that there would be no evil in a low qualification. It can hardly be said, however, on the other hand, that there would be any good; for if the whole mass of the people who have some property would make a good choice, it will hardly be pretended that, added to them, the comparatively small number of those who have none, and whose minds are naturally and almost necessarily governed by the minds of those who have, would be able to make the choice a bad one.

We have ascertained, therefore, two points. We have ascertained that a very low qualification is of no use, as affording no security for a good choice beyond that which would exist if no pecuniary qualification was required. We have likewise ascertained, that a qualification so high as to constitute an Aristocracy of wealth, though it were a very numerous one, would leave the community without protection, and exposed to all the evils of unbridled power. The only question, therefore, is, whether, between these extremes, there is any qualification which would remove the right of Suffrage from the people of small, or of no property, and yet constitute an elective body, the interest of which would be identical with that of the community?

It is not easy to find any satisfactory principle to guide us in our researches, and to tell us where we should fix. The qualification must either be such as to embrace the majority of the population, or some thing less than the majority. Suppose, in the first place, that it embraces the majority, the question is, whether the majority would have an interest in oppressing those who, upon this supposition, would be deprived of political power? If we reduce the calculation to its elements, we shall see that the interest which they would have, of this deplorable kind, though it would be something, would not be very great. Each man of the majority, if the majority were constituted the governing body, would have something less than the benefit of oppressing a single man. If the majority were twice as great as the minority, each man of the majority would only have one-half the benefit of oppressing a single man. In that case, the benefits of good Government, accruing to all, might be expected to overbalance to the several members of such an elective body the benefits of misrule peculiar to themselves. Good Government, would, therefore, have a tolerable security. Suppose, in the second place, that the qualification did not admit a body of electors so large as the majority, in that case, taking again the calculation in its elements, we shall see that each man would have a benefit equal to that derived from the oppression of more than one man; and that, in proportion as the elective body constituted a smaller and smaller minority, the benefit of misrule to the elective body would be increased, and bad Government would be insured.

It seems hardly necessary to carry the analysis of the pecuniary qualification, as the principle for choosing an elective body, any farther.

We have only remaining the third plan for constituting an elective body. According to the scheme in question, the best elective body is that which consists of certain classes, professions, or fraternities. The notion is, that when these fraternities or bodies are represented, the community itself is represented. The way in which, according to the patrons of this theory, the effect is brought about, is this. Though it is perfectly true, that each of these fraternities would profit by misrule, and have the strongest interest in promoting it; yet, if three or four such fraternities are appointed to act in conjunction, they will not profit by misrule, and will have an interest in nothing but good Government.

This theory of Representation we shall not attempt to trace farther back than the year 1793. In the debate on the motion of Mr (now Earl) Grey, for a Reform in the System of Representation, on the 6th of May, of that year, Mr Jenkinson, the present Earl of Liverpool, brought forward this theory of Representation, and urged it in opposition to all idea of Reform in the British House of Commons, in terms as clear and distinct as those in which it has recently been clothed by leading men on both sides of that House. We shall transcribe the passage from the speech of Mr Jenkinson, omitting, for the sake of abbreviation, all those expressions which are unnecessary for

4-2

conveying a knowledge of the plan, and of the reasons upon which it was founded.

"Supposing it agreed", he said, "that the House of Commons is meant to be a legislative body, representing all descriptions of men in the country, he supposed every person would agree, that the landed interest ought to have the preponderant weight. The landed interest was, in fact, the *stamina* of the country. In the second place, in a commercial country like this, the manufacturing and commercial interest ought to have a considerable weight, secondary to the landed interest, but secondary to the landed interest only. But was this all that was necessary? There were other descriptions of people, which, to distinguish them from those already mentioned, he should style professional people, and whom he considered as absolutely necessary to the composition of a House of Commons. By professional people, he meant those Members of the House of Commons who wished to raise themselves to the great offices of the State; those that were in the army, those that were in the navy, those that were in the law." He then, as a reason for desiring to have those whom he calls "professional people" in the composition of the House of Commons, gives it as a fact, that country Gentlemen and Merchants seldom desire, and seldom have motives for desiring, to be Ministers and other great Officers of State. These Ministers and Officers, however, ought to be made out of the House of Commons. Therefore, you ought to have "professional people" of whom to make them. Nor was this all. "There was another reason why these persons were absolutely necessary. We were constantly in the habit of discussing in that House all the important concerns of the State. It was necessary, therefore, that there should be persons in the practice of debating such questions." "There was a third reason, which, to his mind, was stronger than all the rest. Suppose that in that House there were only country Gentlemen, they would not then be the Representatives of the nation, but of the landholders. Suppose there were in that House only commercial persons, they would not be the Representatives of the nation, but of the commercial interest of the nation. Suppose the landed and commercial interest could both find their way into the House. The landed interest would be able, if it had nothing but the commercial interest to combat with, to prevent that interest from having its due weight in the Constitution. All descriptions of persons in the country would thus, in fact, be at the mercy of the landholders." He adds, "the professional persons are, then, what makes this House the Representatives of the people. They have collectively no *esprit de corps*, and prevent any *esprit de*

53

corps from affecting the proceedings of the House. Neither the landed nor commercial interest can materially affect each other, and the interests of the different professions of the country are fairly considered. The Honourable Gentleman (Mr Grey), and the petition on this table, rather proposed uniformity of election. His ideas were the reverse—that the modes of election ought to be as varied as possible, because, if there was but one mode of election, there would, generally speaking, be but one description of persons in that House, and by a varied mode of election only could that variety be secured."

There is great vagueness undoubtedly in the language here employed; and abundant wavering and uncertainty in the ideas. But the ideas regarding this theory, appear in the same half-formed state in every speech and writing in which we have seen it adduced. The mist, indeed, by which it has been kept surrounded, alone creates the difficulty; because it cannot be known precisely how any thing is good or bad, till it is precisely known what it is.

According to the ideas of Lord Liverpool, the landholders ought to be represented; the merchants and manufacturers ought to be represented; the officers of the army and navy ought to be represented; and the practitioners of the law ought to be represented. Other patrons of the scheme have added, that literary men ought to be represented. And these, we believe, are almost all the fraternities which have been named for this purpose by any of the advocates of representation by clubs. To insure the choice of Representatives of the landholders, landholders must be the choosers; to insure the choice of Representatives of the merchants and manufacturers, merchants and manufacturers must be the choosers; and so with respect to the other fraternities, whether few or many. Thus it must be at least in *substance*; whatever the *form*, under which the visible acts may be performed. According to the scheme in question, these several fraternities are represented *directly*, the rest of the community is *not* represented directly; but it will be said by the patrons of that scheme, that it is represented *virtually*, which, in this case, answers the same purpose.

From what has already been ascertained, it will appear certain, that each of these fraternities has its sinister interest, and will be led to seek the benefit of misrule, if it is able to obtain it. This is frankly and distinctly avowed by Lord Liverpool. And by those by whom it is not avowed, it seems impossible to suppose that it should be disputed.

Let us now, then, observe the very principle upon which this theory must be supported. Three, or four, or five, or more clubs of men, have unlimited power over the whole community put into their hands. These clubs have, each, and all of them, an interest, an interest the same with that which governs all other rulers, in misgovernment, in converting the persons and properties of the rest of the community wholly to their own benefit. Having this interest, says the theory, they will not make use of it, but will use all their powers for the benefit of the community. Unless this proposition can be supported, the theory is one of the shallowest by which the pretenders to political wisdom have ever exposed themselves.

Let us resume the proposition. Three, or four, or five fraternities of men, composing a small part of the community, have all the powers of government placed in their hands. If they oppose and contend with one another, they will be unable to convert these powers to their own benefit. If they agree they will be able to convert them wholly to their own benefit, and to do with the rest of the community just what they please. The patrons of this system of Representation assume, that these fraternities will be sure to take that course which is *contrary* to their interest. The course which is *according* to their interest, appears as if it had never presented itself to their imaginations !

There being two courses which the clubs may pursue, one contrary to their interest, the other agreeable to it, the patrons of the club system

56

must prove, they must place it beyond all doubt, that the clubs will follow the first course, and not follow the second: if not, the world will laugh at a theory which is founded upon a direct contradiction of one of the fundamental principles of human nature.

In supposing that clubs or societies of men are governed, like men individually, by their interests, we are surely following a pretty complete experience. In the idea that a certain number of those clubs can unite to pursue a common interest, there is surely nothing more extraordinary, than that as many individuals should unite to pursue a common interest. Lord Liverpool talks of an *esprit de corps* belonging to a class of landholders, made up of the different bodies of landholders in every county in the kingdom. He talks of an *esprit de corps* in a class of merchants and manufacturers, made up of the different bodies of merchants and manufacturers in the several great towns and manufacturing districts in the kingdom. What, then, is meant by an *esprit de corps*? Nothing else but a union for the pursuit of a common interest. To the several clubs supposed in the present theory, a common interest is created by the very circumstance of their composing the representing and represented bodies. Unless the patrons of this theory can prove to us, contrary to all experience, that a common interest cannot create an *esprit de corps* in men in combinations, as well as in men individually, we are under the necessity of believing, that an *esprit de corps* would be formed in the classes separated from the rest of the community for the purposes of Representation; that they would pursue their common interest; and inflict all the evils upon the rest of the community to which the pursuit of that interest would lead.

It is not included in the idea of this union for the pursuit of a common interest, that the clubs or sets of persons appropriated to the business of Representation should totally harmonize. There would, no doubt, be a great mixture of agreement and disagreement among them. But there would, if experience is any guide, or if the general laws of human nature have any power, be sufficient agreement to prevent their losing sight of the common interest; in other words, for insuring all that abuse of power which is useful to the parties by whom it is exercised.

The real effect of this motley Representation, therefore, would only be to create a motley Aristocracy; and, of course, to insure that kind of misgovernment which it is the nature of Aristocracy to produce, and to produce equally, whether it is a uniform, or a variegated Aristocracy; whether an Aristocracy all of landowners; or an Aristocracy in part landowners, in part merchants and manufacturers, in part officers of the army and navy, and in part lawyers.

We have now, therefore, examined the principles of the Representative system, and have found in it all that is necessary to constitute a security for good government: We have seen in what manner it is possible to prevent in the Representatives the rise of an interest different from that of the parties who choose them, namely, by giving them little time, not dependent upon the will of those parties: We have likewise seen in what manner identity of interest may be insured between the electoral body and the rest of the community: We have, therefore, discovered the means by which identity of interest may be insured between the Representatives and the community at large. We have, by consequence, obtained an organ of Government which possesses that quality, without which there can be no good Government.

I. *Objection: That a perfect Representative System, if established, would destroy the Monarchy, and the House of Lords*

The question remains, Whether this organ is competent to the performance of the whole of the business of Government? And it may be certainly answered, that it is not. It may be competent to the making of laws, and it may watch over their execution: but to the executive functions themselves, operations in detail, to be performed by individuals, it is manifestly not competent. The executive functions of Government consist of two parts, the administrative and the judicial. The administrative, in this country, belong to the King; and it will appear indubitable, that, if the best mode of disposing of the administrative powers of Government be to place them in the hands of one great functionary, not elective, but hereditary; a King, such as ours, instead of being inconsistent with the Representative system, in its highest state of perfection, would be an indispensable branch of a good Government; and, even if it did not previously exist, would be established by a Representative body whose interests were identified, as above, with those of the nation.

The same reasoning will apply exactly to our House of Lords. Suppose it true, that, for the perfect performance of the business of Legislation, and of watching over the execution of the laws, a second deliberative Assembly is necessary; and that an Assembly, such as the British House of Lords, composed of the proprietors of the greatest landed estates, with dignities and privileges, is the best adapted to the end: it follows, that a body of Representatives, whose interests were identified with those of the nation, would establish such an Assembly, if it did not previously exist: for the best of all possible reasons; that they would have motives for, and none at all against it.

Those parties, therefore, who reason against any measures necessary for identifying the interests of the Representative body with those of the nation, under the plea that such a Representative body would abolish the King and the House of Lords, are wholly inconsistent with themselves. They maintain that a King and a House of Lords, such as ours, are important and necessary branches of a good Government. It is demonstratively certain that a Representative body, the interests of which were identified with those of the nation, would have no motive to abolish them, if they were not causes of bad government. Those persons, therefore, who affirm that it would certainly abolish them, affirm implicitly that they are causes of bad, and not necessary to good government. This oversight of theirs is truly surprising.

The whole of this chain of deduction is dependent, as we stated at the beginning, upon the principle that the acts of men will be conformable to their interests. Upon this principle, we conceive that the chain is complete and irrefragable. The principle, also, appears to stand upon a strong foundation. It is indisputable that the acts of men follow their will; that their will follows their desires; and that their desires are generated by their apprehensions of good or evil; in other words, by their interests.

X

II. *Objection: That the People are not capable of acting agreeably to their Interest*

The apprehensions of the people, respecting good and evil, may be just, or they may be erroneous. If just, their actions will be agreeable to their real interests. If erroneous, they will not be agreeable to their real interests, but to a false supposition of interest.

We have seen, that, unless the Representative Body are chosen by a portion of the community the interest of which cannot be made to differ from that of the community, the interest of the community will infallibly be sacrificed to the interest of the rulers.

The whole of that party of reasoners who support Aristocratical power affirm, that a portion of the community, the interest of whom cannot be made to differ from that of the community, will not act according to their interest, but contrary to their interest. All their pleas are grounded upon this assumption. Because, if a portion of the community whose interest is the same with that of the community, would act agreeably to their own interest, they would act agreeably to the interest of the community, and the end of Government would be obtained.

If this assumption of theirs is true, the prospect of mankind is deplorable. To the evils of misgovernment they are subject by inexorable destiny. If the powers of Government are placed in the hands of persons whose interests are not identified with those of the community, the interests of the community are wholly sacrificed to those of the rulers. If so much as a checking power is held by the community, or by any part of the community, where the interests are the same as those of the community, the holders of that checking power will not, according to the assumption in question, make use of it in a way agreeable, but in a way contrary to their own interest. According to this theory, the choice is placed between the evils which will be produced by design, the design of those who have the power of oppressing the rest of the community, and an interest in doing it; and the evils which may be produced by mistake, the mistake of those who, if they acted agreeably to their own interest, would act well.

Supposing that this theory were true, it would still be a question, between these two sets of evils, whether the evils arising from the design of those who have motives to employ the powers of Government for the purpose of reducing the community to the state of abject slaves of their will, or the evils arising from the misconduct of those who never produce evil but when they mistake their own interest, are the greatest evils.

Upon the most general and summary view of this question, it appears that the proper answer cannot be doubtful. They who have a fixed, invariable interest in acting ill, will act ill invariably. They who act ill from mistake, will often act well, sometimes even by accident, and in every case in which they are enabled to understand their interest, by design.

There is another, and a still more important ground of preference. The evils which are the produce of interest and power united, the evils on the one side, are altogether incurable: the effects are certain while that conjunction which is the cause of them remains. The evils which arise from mistake are not incurable; for, if the parties who act contrary to their interest had a proper knowledge of that interest, they would act well. What is necessary, then, is knowledge. Knowledge, on the part of those whose interests are the same as those of the community, would be an adequate remedy. But knowledge is a thing which is capable of being increased: and the more it is increased the more the evils on this side of the case would be reduced.

Supposing, then, the theory of will opposed to interest to be correct, the practical conclusion would be, as there is something of a remedy to the evils arising from this source, none whatever to the evils arising from the conjunction of power and sinister interest, to adopt the side which has the remedy, and to do whatever is necessary for obtaining the remedy in its greatest possible strength, and for applying it with the greatest possible efficacy.

It is no longer deniable that a high degree of knowledge is capable of being conveyed to such a portion of the community, as would have interests the same with those of the community. This being the only resource for good government, those who say that it is not yet attained stand in this dilemma; either they do not desire good government, which is the case with all those who derive advantage from bad; or they will be seen employing their utmost exertions to increase the quantity of knowledge in the body of the community.

The practical conclusion, then, is actually the same, whether we embrace or reject the assumption that the community are little capable of acting according to their own interest.

That assumption, however, deserves to be considered. And it would need a more minute consideration than the space to which we are confined will enable us to bestow upon it.

One caution, first of all, we should take along with us; and it is this, That all those persons who hold the powers of Government, without having an identity of interests with the community, and all those persons who share in the profits which are made by the abuse of those powers, and all those persons whom the example and representations of the two first classes influence, will be sure to represent the community, or a part having an identity of interest with the community, as incapable in the highest degree, of acting according to their own interest; it being clear that they who have not an identity of interest with the community, ought to hold the power of Government no longer, if those who have that identity of interest could be expected to act in any tolerable conformity with their interest. All representations from that quarter, therefore, of their incapability so to act, are to be received with suspicion. They come from interested parties; they come from parties who have the strongest possible interest to deceive themselves, and to endeavour to deceive others.

It is impossible that the interested endeavours of all those parties should not propagate, and for a long time successfully uphold, such an opinion, to whatever degree it might be found, upon accurate inquiry, to be without foundation.

67

A parallel case may be given. It was the interest of the priesthood, when the people of Europe were all of one religion, that the laity should take their opinions exclusively from them; because, in that case, the laity might be rendered subservient to the will of the Clergy, to any possible extent; and as all opinions were to be derived professedly from the Bible, they withdrew from the laity the privilege of reading it. When the opinions which produced the Reformation, and all the blessings which may be traced to it, began to ferment, the privilege of the Bible was demanded. The demand was resisted by the Clergy, upon the very same assumption which we have now under contemplation. "The people did not understand their own interest. They would be sure to make a bad use of the Bible. They would derive from it not right opinions, but all sorts of wrong opinions."*

There can be no doubt that the assumption, in the religious case, was borne out by still stronger appearance of evidence, than it is in the political. The majority of the people may be supposed less capable of deriving correct opinions from the Bible, than of judging who is the best man to act as a Representative.

* A most instructive display of these and similar artifices for the preservation of mischievous power, after the spirit of the times is felt to be hostile to it, may be seen in Father Paul's *History of the Council of Trent.*

Experience has fully displayed the nature of the assumption in regard to religion. The power bestowed upon the people, of judging for themselves, has been productive of good effects, to a degree which has totally altered the condition of human nature, and exalted man to what may be called a different stage of existence.

For what reason then, is it, we are called upon to believe, that, if a portion of the community, having an identity of interests with the whole community, have the power of choosing Representatives, they will act wholly contrary to their interests, and make a bad choice?

Experience, it will be said, establishes this conclusion. We see that the people do not act according to their interests, but very often in opposition to them.

The question is between a portion of the community, which, if entrusted with power, would have an interest in making a bad use of it, and a portion which, though entrusted with power, would not have an interest in making a bad use of it. The former are any small number whatsoever; who, by the circumstance of being entrusted with power, are constituted an Aristocracy.

From the frequency, however great, with which those who compose the mass of the community act in opposition to their interests, no conclusion can, in this case, be drawn, without a comparison of the frequency with which those, who are placed in contrast with them, act in opposition to theirs. Now, it may with great confidence be affirmed, that as great a proportion of those who compose the Aristocratical body of any country, as of those who compose the rest of the community, are distinguished for a conduct unfavourable to their interests. Prudence is a more general characteristic of the people who are without the advantages of fortune, than of the people who have been thoroughly subject to their corruptive operation. It may surely be said, that if the powers of Government must be entrusted to persons incapable of good conduct, they were better entrusted to incapables who have an interest in good government, than to incapables who have an interest in bad.

It will be said that a conclusion ought not to be drawn from the unthinking conduct of the great majority of an Aristocratical body, against the capability of such a body for acting wisely in the management of public affairs; because the body will always contain a certain proportion of wise men, and the rest will be governed by them. Nothing but this can be said with pertinency. And, under certain modifications, this may be said with truth. The wise and good in any class of men do, to all general purposes, govern the rest. The comparison, however, must go on. Of that body, whose interests are identified with those of the community, it may also be said, that if one portion of them are unthinking, there is another portion wise; and that, in matters of state, the less wise would be governed by the more wise, not less certainly than in that body, whose interests, if they were entrusted with power, could not be identified with those of the community.

If we compare in each of these two contrasted bodies the two descriptions of persons, we shall not find that the foolish part of the Democratical body are more foolish than that of the Aristocratical, nor the wise part less wise.

Though, according to the opinions which fashion has propagated, it may appear a little paradoxical, we shall probably find the very reverse.

That there is not only as great a proportion of wise men in that part of the community which is not the Aristocracy, as in that which is; but that, under the present state of education, and the diffusion of knowledge, there is a much greater, we presume, there are few persons who will be disposed to dispute. It is to be observed, that the class which is universally described as both the most wise and the most virtuous part of the community, the middle rank, are wholly included in that part of the community which is not the Aristocratical. It is also not disputed, that in

Great Britain the middle rank are numerous, and form a large proportion of the whole body of the people. Another proposition may be stated, with a perfect confidence of the concurrence of all those men who have attentively considered the formation of opinions in the great body of society, or, indeed, the principles of human nature in general. It is, that the opinions of that class of the people, who are below the middle rank, are formed, and their minds are directed by that intelligent and virtuous rank, who come the most immediately in contact with them, who are in the constant habit of intimate communication with them, to whom they fly for advice and assistance in all their numerous difficulties, upon whom they feel an immediate and daily dependence, in health and in sickness, in infancy and in old age; to whom their children look up as models for their imitation, whose opinions they hear daily repeated, and account it their honour to adopt. There can be no doubt that the middle rank, which gives to science, to art, and to legislation itself, their most distinguished ornaments, the chief source of all that has exalted and refined human nature, is that portion of the community of which, if the basis of Representation were ever so far extended, the opinion would ultimately decide. Of the people beneath them, a vast majority would be sure to be guided by their advice and example.

The incidents which have been urged as exceptions to this general rule, and even as reasons for rejecting it, may be considered as contributing to its proof. What signify the irregularities of a mob, more than half composed, in the greater number of instances, of boys and women, and disturbing, for a few hours or days, a particular town? What signifies the occasional turbulence of a manufacturing district, peculiarly unhappy from a very great deficiency of a middle rank, as there the population almost wholly consists of rich manufacturers and poor workmen; with whose minds no pains are taken by anybody; with whose afflictions there is no virtuous family of the middle rank to sympathize; whose children have no good example of such a family to see and to admire; and who are placed in the highly unfavourable situation of fluctuating between very high wages in one year, and very low wages in another? It is altogether futile with regard to the foundation of good government to say that this or the other portion of the people, may at this, or the other time, depart from the wisdom of the middle rank. It is enough that the great majority of the people never cease to be guided by that rank; and we may, with some confidence, challenge the adversaries of the people to produce a single instance to the contrary in the history of the world.

For EU product safety concerns, contact us at Calle de José Abascal, 56–1°, 28003 Madrid, Spain or eugpsr@cambridge.org.

www.ingramcontent.com/pod-product-compliance
Ingram Content Group UK Ltd.
Pitfield, Milton Keynes, MK11 3LW, UK
UKHW012327130625
459647UK00009B/116